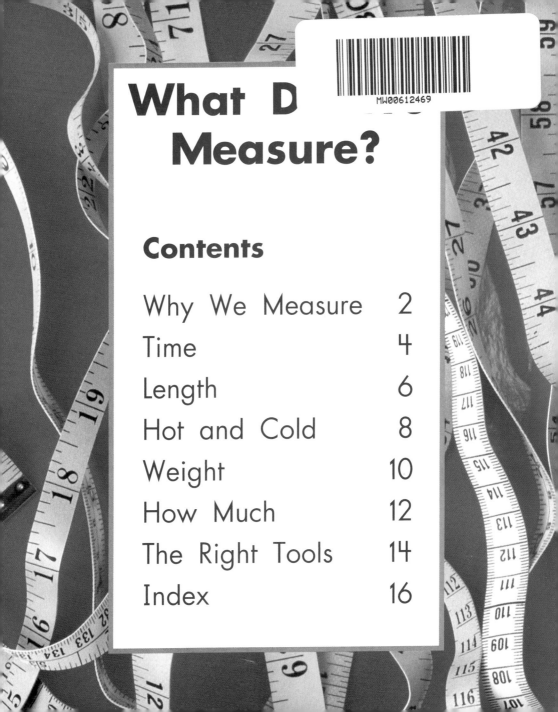

# What D... Measure?

## Contents

# Why We Measure

How are a ruler, a cup,
and a clock the same?
We use them all to measure.

2

We need to measure
different things
every day.

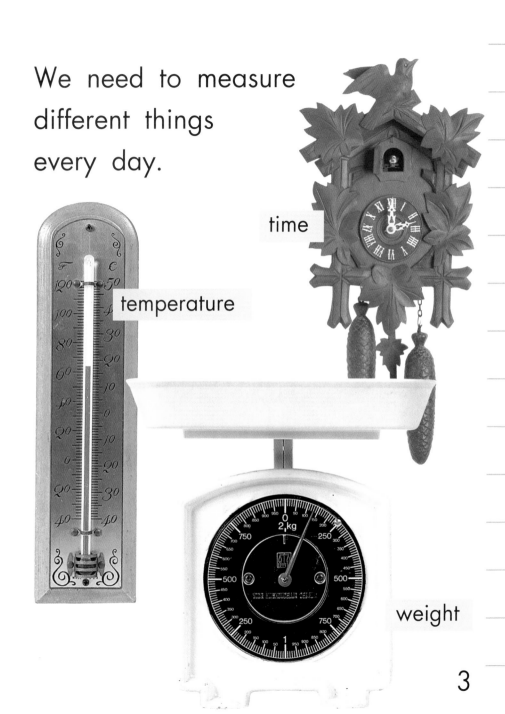

time

temperature

weight

3

# Time

Clocks measure time. They tell us when we need to wake up.

They tell us when it is time for lunch.

They tell us when we need to go to bed.

# Length

We measure how tall we are.

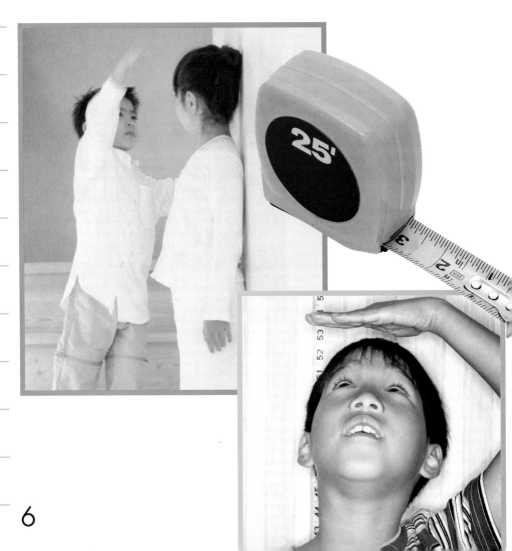

# We measure how far we jump.

Measuring tapes and rulers measure length.

# Hot and Cold

We measure how hot or cold it is outside.

Temperature is measured in degrees.

We measure how hot
it is in the oven.

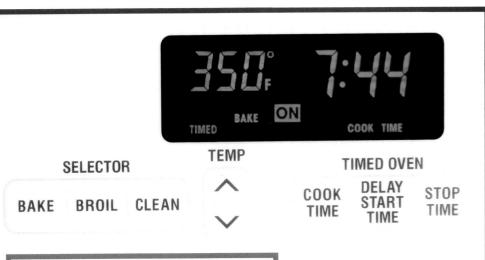

Thermometers
measure
temperature.

9

# Weight

We measure how heavy we are.

We measure how heavy food is.

We measure how heavy
letters are.

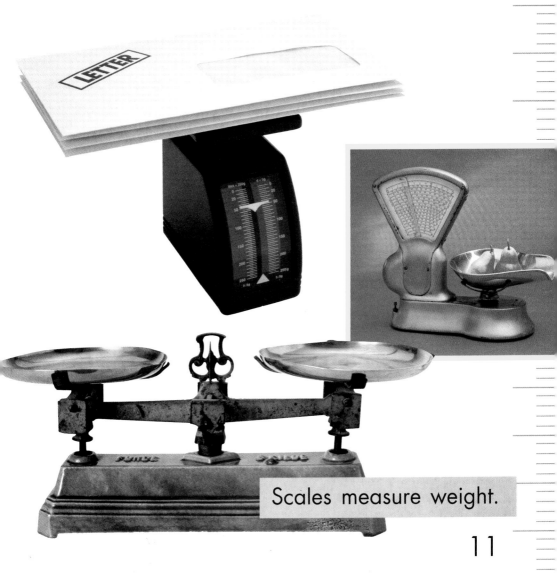

Scales measure weight.

# How Much

We measure when we bake.

Measuring cups and spoons measure how much of something.

For liquids: fill the cup to the line for the amount you need.

For dry foods: fill the cup to the top and scrape off the extra.

# The Right Tools

It is important to use
the right tool
when we measure.
A ruler can't tell us
how heavy something is!

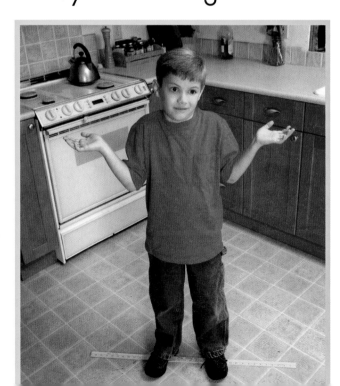

A clock can't tell us
how much milk to use
when we cook!

**Measuring tips**

When you measure:
- use the right tools.
- be accurate.

# Index